Thanksgiving is near!

I board a huge plane,
fly up and away!
My cousins are there.
I can't wait to play.

Our suitcases drop.
Front door opens wide.
My parents get kisses,
we kids sneak outside.

I help to clean up
and get ready to cook.
Out from the top drawer
comes our recipe book.

Just like long ago,
Mama says we will share
good food and kindness
to show that we care.

I go with my mom
to our general store.
We fill our cart full,
but there's still room for more.

She peeks down the rows
and finds a surprise:
an apron for helping,
with extra-long ties!

$2

cauliflower

$.50

I am thankful.

My heart grows.

Love fills me

from head to toes!

We load into cars
and drive many miles.
The patch is so full
of long pumpkin aisles.

I climb in the wagon,
and sit on hay seats.
The farmer's lips whistle
as he drives through the streets.

Grandma makes pies.
The rolling pin spins.
We pat the dough softly
into the round tins.

The filling's so creamy
with spices just right.
Still warm from the oven,
she gives me a bite.

Today for a craft
I lay my hand flat,
trace around fingers:
a turkey place mat!

Art for our table
with scissors and glue,
some crayons and pens—
I'll make a card, too.

I am thankful.

My heart grows.

Love fills me

from head to toes!

It's old picture time.
I run to the shelf,
stand on my tiptoes,
and reach them myself.

Albums and boxes
of such happy faces,
pictures of birthdays,
and trips to cool places.

Big brother is home
from school far away.
I missed him so much,
I've waited all day.

We pick out a puzzle
and sit on the floor.
I dump out the pieces,
three hundred or more!

A knock at the door,
it's time for our trip—
a hike through the park!
Grab water to sip.

Slow careful steps,

through tall golden trees.

We find a leaf pile

and drop to our knees.

I am thankful.

My heart grows.

Love fills me

from head to toes!

Time for the parade.
We gather around.
Balloons fill the sky,
feet march on the ground.

I grab the remote,
and switch to football.
Then over to doggies,
some big and some small.

Collecting some extra
treats we can spare,
I look through the pantry
to see what's in there.

We drop off big bags
of green beans and corn.
The clerk stacks the cans.
His gloves are all worn.

The phone sings its tone,
I can tell that it's Dad.
We each take turns sharing
the days that we've had.

He tells me, "Love you.
And remember, behave."
I tell him, "You, too.
Stay safe and be brave."

I am thankful.

My heart grows.

Love fills me

from head to toes!

The kitchen is busy.

I grab the soup bowls,

count the cloth napkins,

my nose smells the rolls.

The table is ready.

We each have a seat.

Hands held so tightly,

we're ready to eat.

Whisking and basting,
we each do our part.
Buffet line gets longer,
I can't wait to start!

Our guests will arrive,
not a moment too soon.
"Grab a clean plate,
and a knife, fork, and spoon!"

We go to serve folks
with smiles so bright.
Their trays piled high,
eyes shine with delight.

When tummies are full
and buttons are snug,
I move seat to seat
to pass out some hugs.

I am thankful.
My heart grows.
Love fills me
from head to toes!

Family and friends
with grins ear to ear,
all gathered together–
Thanksgiving is here!

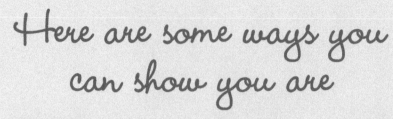

Here are some ways you can show you are

thankful!

MAKE AN "I AM THANKFUL" POSTER

Use the words below to draw and decorate a poster for your room to remind you to give thanks at this special time of year—and all year long!

I am thankful.
My Heart grows.
Love fills me
from Head to toes!

DRAW AND PASS OUT THANK-YOU CARDS

Give cards to people you don't usually thank, like a grocery store clerk, the postal carrier, or a waiter at a restaurant, to show them you appreciate the hard work they do for you. Remember: Always ask an adult for permission and supervision before handing out cards or sending anything to anyone.

MAKE YOUR OWN THANKFUL TURKEY PLACE MATS

Trace your hand on paper and color with crayons and markers, or add paper cutouts, yarn, or stickers. Write "I am thankful for" along the top of the paper. Along the bottom, draw a blank line "_____" so each person can fill it in with something special.

MAKE A FAMILY THANKFULNESS TREE

Cut out leaves from colored paper. Get a branch from outside and place it in a vase. Give each family member two leaves to write their name on one side, and something or someone they are thankful for on the other side. Hang the leaves on the branch with ribbon or paper clips.

PLAY THE THANKFULNESS COUNTDOWN

Slide a number under every plate at the table. Have each person find their number and, in order from the highest to the lowest number, invite them to share a memory about feeling thankful. The person who shares first also gets to be served dessert first!

SHERI WALL is a lover of rhyme who has lived in Texas for a really long time. She would read to her sons and kids that she knew, and they all enjoyed rhyming picture books, too. Then *A Matter of Rhyme* began as a dream to help others learn with zippy rhyme schemes. Sheri likes to stay active and be on the go, either biking, shopping, or seeing a show. To find more lively books by this witty mom, visit her website, amatterofrhyme.com.

HOLLY CLIFTON-BROWN is an illustrator and artist based in Somerset, England. She graduated from the University of the West of England (UWE Bristol) in 2008, and has since published several picture books and illustrations for an array of international publishing companies and clients. Her work combines traditional painting, mixed media, and collage with contemporary techniques to create a unique and imaginative visual language. When Holly is not drawing, you'll find her in the bath tub, out walking in the countryside with her family, fermenting vegetables, and having micro adventures with her two children and dog, Olive.